Things
I Never Want
To Forget

Things
I Never Want
To Forget

Don C. Allen

Things I Never Want To Forget

Copyright Year: 2007
Copyright Notice: by Don C. Allen. All rights reserved.

Results in this copyright notice:

FIRST EDITION

ISBN 978-0-6151-5474-9

Dedication

A man that hath friends must shew himself friendly:
and there is a friend that sticketh closer than a brother.
Proverbs 18:24

I have been blessed to have found a beautiful wife in Christina
and to have been given three truly amazing children in
Bethany, Zach, and Jordan.

My Parents and extended family
are a great treasure in my life.

But in dedication of this book I want to honor one
who has helped me understand the above Scripture.

At first this Scripture was a mystery to me
as people spoke of the betrayal of a brother,
but then I came to realize that was not the true meaning at all.

There is a closeness that comes from a brother
that cannot be easily put into words.

My brother has been a protector, provider, and a teacher.
You are truly a nail providing a sure place.

It is with gratitude that I dedicate this book to my
Big Brother
Scott

Contents

Foreword

Things I Never Want To Forget by Pastor Don Allen is one of the most enjoyable, inspiring, encouraging and faith building books I have read in a long time. I started and finished the book in one day because I could not put it down.

Pastor Allen draws from his rich background as evangelist, church planter, and pastor and also his experiences in multicultural and international ministries.

He gives the reader a glimpse into the real life and work of a minister. He pierces the façade and image of the minister by sharing his own experiences of spiritual warfare with the enemy of our souls and despite times of anxieties and doubts, how God teaches him with each experience and performs miracle after miracle to affirm time and again that God is on the Throne and is working daily in our lives even when we don't always recognize him.

These profound and miraculous experiences are so powerful and are etched so indelibly in the mind and heart of this pastor and are so special to him until he wants to share them with everybody.

The reader will see the heart of this man. You will see the compassion he has for people and the passion he has for God. You will discover why he is such a successful pastor. The real life stories and accounts of God's work in the life of believers are so gripping that it will impact your own faith and strengthen your resolve for the challenges of what you are facing at the moment and for the future.

The book is both earthy and heavenly. It is earthy as it deals with the pain, upheavals, disappointments, sickness, bereavement, challenges, and humanity that confronts a minister in his call to love and care for his congregation/community as well as his own personal challenges in carrying out the mandate of the Gospel; the mandate in caring and shepherding the flock God has placed in his care, but also in fulfilling the Divine Commission to "go into all the world and preach the Gospel to every creature...."

Pastor Allen is very transparent throughout the book. He never attempts to glorify and romanticize the ministry or to ascend to a pedestal for personal aggrandizement. He shares with the reader about real people and real situations. The reader can identify with a particular situation somewhere in the book because all have, at some time or other, walked down that particular road.

The book is also heavenly in that it ushers the reader into the very Throne room and presence of God. It seems that Pastor Allen keeps the hand of the reader in one hand and the hand of God in the other.

There are times you will weep and times you will rejoice and times when the overpowering presence of the Holy Spirit will sweep you away and above your own problems into the realization that God is still on His Throne and is in control of your life and situation.

In this book, you are an eyewitness as it were to the miraculous; Miracles of healings that neither man nor science can explain away; Miracles of deliverance and Divine protection; Miracles where God speaks and every time God confirms His message; Miracles of provisions when the meal barrel is empty and the car payment is due and God provides just as He declares in his Word.

This book will remind you that God is the same today as He has always been and that His arm isn't shortened. Just as

He healed yesterday, He will heal today. Just as he caused the lame to walk yesterday, He will do it today. Just as men and women on the precipice of death were raised up to life yesterday, He will do it again today. Just as God rained manna from heaven to the children of Israel yesterday, God will supply food and raiment and blessings today.

Pastor Allen draws from his own personal experiences from a young evangelist to a highly successful pastor whose ministry is in demand around the world. He uses a fresh and easy to read writing style that is captivating.

The contents of the book are testimonies of events so powerful and memorable that the author states he will never forget them. This book will build your faith and will be a book that, like the title, you will never forget. It will quickly become one of your all time favorites. A must read.

Robert White,
International Evangelist

Introduction

EING A MAN of above average size, I usually avoid tight and uncomfortable places, but upon this night I found myself in just that – a tight and uncomfortable place. I was crammed into a seat between others crammed into their seats waiting for a concert to begin. Then the music began and it was excruciatingly loud. It was the type of loud you feel in your body before you actually hear any sounds. I say "sounds" because there wasn't much melody to it, just a driving rhythm to which everyone but me was responding. People across the crowd moved in unison to the music. I was the lone unmoving pillar in the middle because I can't even clap in church, much less "boogie" with the best of Atlanta's contemporary Christian crowd. I asked myself, "Why am I here? I don't even like concerts!" Then, in the blink of an eye, I clearly remembered my purpose. I scanned the crowd and about twenty rows ahead of me on the floor of Atlanta's famous Fox Theatre, I caught a glimpse of the top of a familiar head bobbing up and down to the music. The top of that bushy-haired head, and all the rest that was attached, made up a man that God had brought into my life some years earlier.

He first entered my life as a "don't lay a hand on me" type of guy who was big and tough enough to enforce his reserved and stand-offish nature. He would come to church and then go home and "get high" to process what he'd heard. Over the years, I have seen people search in many places to find peace and meaning in life. Some rely entirely on their own abilities for fulfillment and only look within themselves, while others search through many alternatives. In spite of where their search takes them, they still long for the peace, joy, fulfillment, and lasting security that only comes through a personal relationship with God. Through his son, Jesus Christ, God offers his love to the whole world. To come to Christ is an invitation to all, and everyone who hears the Gospel of Christ must choose to either accept or reject God's invitation.

One day Frank found the greatest high of all. He called upon the name of Christ, confessed his sins and made heaven his home. He was gloriously saved! From then on, no chemically-induced high could compete with what God had done in him. This change was evidenced by the new smile that now crossed his big, hairy face. However, the biggest change of all was that this once tough, macho man became a tender-hearted, crying, hugging, loveable man. Instead of hiding in the back of the sanctuary, he was now in the front loving on everybody. He enrolled and excelled in the church's School of Ministry. He joined the worship team, bought a guitar and quickly found a place for himself. Finally, he became the worship leader in the children's ministry. This once intimidating man became a favorite teddy bear to the children of our church.

While delighting in my fond memories about this special friend of mine, the concert grabbed my attention once again as the opening act finished. There are very few reasons why I would miss a special service at our church and a concert is definitely not one of them! But this man is very dear to me, and because of him, I find myself at Atlanta's Fox Theatre tonight.

This journey began with a telephone call just a year earlier on a busy morning. That call led to an emergency meeting that changed my life, a meeting I never want to forget. As I left that meeting, I was totally overwhelmed with gratefulness to God because I have been privileged to witness so many great things that He has done. Suddenly, my mind was flooded with people and stories that I never want to forget.

That experience became the inspiration for this book. I believe these are wonderful stories too valuable not to be shared. I pray you will also be inspired and awed by the greatness of Almighty God in these memorable stories of

Things I Never Want To Forget.

Then they that feared the LORD
spake often one to another:
and the LORD hearkened, and heard it, and
<u>a book of remembrance was written</u>
before him for them that feared the LORD,
and that thought upon his name.
Malachi 3:16
(emphasis added)

16

Chapter 1

The Phone Call

I T WAS SHAPING up to be one of those days. Everyone seems to have them. No matter how hard you try, you keep falling farther and farther behind. These are the days when it seems that everyone else needs something and needs it immediately. So, when a pleasant interruption like a phone call from a friend comes through, you smile and feel blessed to have a little break. That's exactly how I was feeling when my two-way radio beeped and I looked down and saw Frank's name. My friend was calling. I knew he was scheduled for a doctor's visit that day and I eagerly anticipated his good news. Frank had been suffering from exhaustion and was having trouble with his basic motor skills. However, I was confident that whatever was wrong could be corrected quickly and I expected him soon to be back to full speed as usual.

When I heard Frank's voice I could tell something was wrong. There are those who can communicate their irritation without actually verbalizing it, while others continue frivolous conversation in an attempt to lead up to their reason for calling. Well, Frank has never been that way. Frank is one of those guys whose voice normally communicates that he is glad to talk. Today, however, his normal excitement about a chance to talk was absent and had been replaced by the sound of a person shocked by some revelation. Frank said one sentence and my schedule instantly cleared. "Pastor, my mom and I need to talk with you as soon as possible."

We quickly arranged to meet at the church. Rarely will I agree to meet with people this quickly because I have learned through difficult experiences that most of these meetings do not go well for a pastor. Typically, a meeting that is scheduled very quickly means that someone only wants to voice their criticism without thinking it through. Usually, people begin by saying how much they love you, but then quickly announce their departure from the church with a critical spirit. But that

18

worry never crossed my mind today because I was confident this meeting would never go in that direction.

I heard them as they arrived and stepped out to greet them. They quickly entered my office and Frank moved right to the point. "Pastor, we have just come from my doctor's office and have been told that I don't have long to live." During times like these, every good pastor has been trained to help an individual and their family move along a specified path of processing and coping with the devastating news they have just received. I asked the questions to begin this process, but the answers I received left me absolutely stunned.

Frank had just been diagnosed with "Lou Gehrig's Disease", the fatal neuromuscular disease Amyotrophic Lateral Sclerosis (ALS), named after the famous New York Yankee baseball player and teammate of Babe Ruth's, who together formed the greatest hitting duo in baseball history until ALS silenced Gehrig's bat as no mortal man ever could.

I knew the prognosis was grim: rapidly increasing paralysis, difficulty in swallowing and speaking, and a short life expectancy. Fear filled my heart. Just a few years earlier, a friend and fellow pastor had been diagnosed with this same disease and within four months he passed away.

Suddenly, I was not just the pastor following the path in which I was trained, but I was a dear friend who was also devastated by this awful diagnosis and prognosis. I was not ready to let Frank go. The three of us wept together.

Frank's thoughts and questions then turned to how his family and friends would handle the news. His concern focused on the little flock he had been leading in children's worship. To this day, tears still flood my eyes every time I remember his words. He reflected, "All my life I have wanted children, and now with this news, I realize I probably will never have any of my own, but I thank God that he has given me forty children at church who have blessed my life." The tears continued as we shared how thankful we were that God had saved Frank and blessed him.

Of course we made no concessions to disease or despair or the enemy. We would fight this to the end, and by faith we would choose to stand on the side of hope. We confessed the Scriptures of healing and we claimed the blessing for health given to us as Christ stood quietly at a whipping post taking stripes upon His back. Our faith was placed in Christ and His promises and not the report of the doctors; and might I add, we still stand upon these promises. Finally, it seemed we were headed down the path of processing this devastating news. However, heaviness still hung in the air.

If there hadn't been enough life-changing moments already during this brief meeting, perhaps I would not have been caught off-guard when it happened. Frank and I had dominated the conversation so there had been little opportunity for the third member of this meeting to participate. Frank's mother is not very big, but it is obvious by the way her children have turned out that she carries a very big stick. She had asked a few questions earlier, but now it was time for her to pull out that "big stick".

Tears were streaming down her cheeks as she started to speak. The tears began to change into a glow. This mother, who had just been told that her son was dying, stared at us both. She lifted her head and as her mouth opened the presence of the living God descended into the room. She made a simple statement that as a young man growing up in church I have heard my whole life. But today her statement of faith was not a "let's just sound spiritual" moment, or even a "my back is hurting and I am pressing through" moment. This was a Paul and Silas moment, a moment when everything within you screams to crawl away and hide. Life had just delivered a beating blow, but from within the prison walls of a "bad diagnosis", her praise of God began to echo. She spoke and the heaviness of sorrow left the room. This mother declared,

"This is the day that the Lord has made,
and I will rejoice and be glad in it."

I sat in stunned silence and then realized my life would never be the same again. I have cried out in my hour of despair

21

and the Lord has heard my cry. I have declared my allegiance to Him even through heartbreak. But on this day I truly saw the locked doors of despair shake loose and open wide by the power of praise. The problem was still real. Medically speaking, we all knew the problem would even grow worse. However, in the midst of this storm, this mother took time to praise God and declare His worthiness; and once again, the waters became peaceful and still.

Chapter 2

Screams In The Night

FOR THOSE WHO have never traveled abroad, the world can seem like a very large place. After several years of traveling through many different countries, I have found it to be exactly the opposite. It's actually rather small. Now, of course, I am not speaking of land mass. Stand on the plains of Africa, overlook the Grand Canyon, or scale the mountains of South America, and it becomes obvious that there is a lot more world still to be discovered. However, in contrast, the world can be small in the way that we are connected to one another. It is not uncommon for me to be upriver in a jungle and run into someone with mutual acquaintances or someone who has heard of my father. The similarity of different cultures is the one common perspective that I believe really brings the world into a much smaller perspective.

Ecclesiastes tells us that God created all men decent, but that it is mankind's pursuit of the indecent that changes him from his original design. Because of mankind's pursuit of evil, men have had to protect themselves not only from animals, but also from other men. As a result, most large cities in every part of the world have two things in common that really stand out: fences and bars.

Fences are built with the thought of keeping in what is treasured and keeping out what is unwelcome. Fences built for the protection of people and properties are built differently than fences built to keep livestock in or out. For protection from mankind, fences are built without space for potential perpetrators to squeeze through.

I have seen this style of fence made out of shrubs with prickly points all over them. One very common fence in Haiti is made of a cactus that is extremely poisonous. Of course, whenever I am around this type of fence I stay as far out of reach as possible. Many times I have been amazed to see toddlers playing within inches of the poisonous spines.

24

The average middle class home in Haiti has a concrete fence that is usually about ten feet high. The fence itself is not the inspiring part, though. It is what tops the fence that catches most eyes. The wealthy top these fences with razor wire. Some will also cement other forms of sharpened metal to the top. However, most use glass bottles and embed a thin layer of broken glass in a thin layer of concrete on top of the wall.

Behind these walls are many different styles of houses, but almost everywhere these houses are concrete. Another common factor between most of the homes is that each one has bars on the windows and steel gates for doors as a second line of defense. I cannot count the times I have heard people beating on a metal gate, trying to get past the outer defenses to enter a home. Most that knock are friendly, and usually they are someone from within who stepped out and became accidentally locked out. One night, however, this was not the case.

It was a muggy December night in Haiti. It's hard to believe that it was muggy at Christmas time. My team and I had just arrived back to Port-au-Prince from the surrounding countryside where we had been teaching the local pastors during the day and ministering to the people of the village during the evening. We were preparing to depart for home the next day. Generally, the day before we leave is uneventful. As usual, this day was no different thus far. While those traveling with me for the first time wanted to souvenir shop and sightsee,

I just wanted to rest and prepare myself for the grueling flights home and the customs inspections at the Miami International Airport. After spending ten days with a host family, all I wanted to do was stay out of their way and let them get back to life without company. With this in mind, my roommate and I headed up to the guest quarters to rest. After an hour or so of reliving the new experiences and miracles we had been privileged to participate in, we finally settled in for some much needed sleep.

On most nights spent away from home, sleep doesn't come easy for me, but on this night I had absolutely no problem falling into a deep sleep. There is a place somewhere between the world of the living and those lost in the grip of slumber where we sometimes feel something is wrong, but are unsure if we are only dreaming or if we should emerge to investigate reality. This is the place where we dream of ringing bells or piercing noises that might take on any form in our dreams, while in reality it is only our alarm clock screaming at us to get up. I believe the key to moving us out of this sluggish state is the persistence of the irritation. Persistence prevailed on this evening.

I was in this place between deep sleep and reality when the screams first started. I thought I heard screams but disregarded them. It was, of course, the middle of the night. Soon I was cognitive of the fact that something was wrong. If

26

you have ever seen a television special on voodoo, you can begin to understand what I was hearing. Drums were beating and people were screaming. Not just the scream of one person or even a small crowd, but the bloodcurdling screams of a drunken mob. The drums seemed to be getting louder with every beat. The outside gate to the house began to rattle. At this point, I realized I was not alone in the room. Sure, my roommate was there, but he was still lost in sound sleep. I wanted to wake him, but what good would that do? If he was going to die, at least death would find him before he knew what hit him. No, there was someone, or something, else in the room — there was a presence.

The crowd outside was not just an angry mob, but a Haitian "Rah Rah", a drunken gathering of people during the holiday season. Instead of celebrating the birth of the Christ Child, these people engage in a wild party based upon a celebration of those who crucified Christ. As the Rah Rah moved down the street, the drunken mob grew in size and violence. Gang wars pale in comparison to the carnage left by the machetes of the Rah Rah.

In my room, I could feel someone breathing down my neck. Chills swept over my body as he began to speak. I should have known that he or one of his forces would have been present. It was just the right atmosphere for this evil presence in my room to become drunk on his own vile

"Where is your God now"
~ mob of anxieties

perversions and begin to torment a child of God. He said, "We will be over the wall soon. We will kill the missionaries, and then we will kill you." He was taunting, laughing, and intimidating, and all the while the screams outside were growing louder. How could anyone hear, much less pray, in this atmosphere? The air was literally heavy with evil.

Often it seems that we wait for a shaft of morning light to break through the darkness and expose our tormentors for the worthless nothings they are, but there was no flash of glory that came to my aid. Even in the darkness of that night, I realized that I did not have to wait for the light to come because the Light had already come into my life. It has been said millions of times, but must be remembered:

> **"Greater is he that is in you,**
> **than he that is in the world."**

From within me strength rose up, and without much fanfare I said, "Oh, it's just you. I rebuke you in the name of Jesus." As if the force of a vacuum was applied, the enemy was instantly sucked from the room. Immediately, his vacated place was filled with a presence of peace and rest. The screams persisted, but for how long I am uncertain, because in the midst of these screams I found one of the most peaceful sleeps I have ever known. Jesus Christ truly had caused me to lie down in green pastures of rest, and before long the screams were replaced with the light of a new day.

28

Chapter 3

A Light
In The Darkness

I HAVE BEEN privileged to travel this globe ministering the Gospel of Jesus Christ. On most of these trips, I am able to discern exactly why I have been sent. Once I was invited to minister in a church a few States over, and when I arrived it was obvious why God had sent me there. This church was going through a devastating legal battle that was very similar to one our church had been through a few years earlier. I was able to speak a brief word of encouragement that their battle would be for them what it had been for us, not a hindrance, but a promotion into greater things in God.

Unfortunately, not every trip has such a clear purpose. Sometimes I find myself very frustrated and quite bewildered as to why I am there. I have found that on every trip people come to Christ, and that makes each struggle worthwhile. Typically, I encounter struggles of being hassled by corrupt immigration officials and being exhausted from travel through overcrowded third world airports with little, if any, air conditioning just to arrive at my destination. Through whatever struggles that come, I have learned to look for that one reason I was chosen for the assignment of presenting the Gospel in this particular corner of the world. Sometimes I find it in the eyes of a small child, a weathered senior, or in groups of people as they receive Christ. Yet, at other times, it is not what I bring that blesses me. It is what I receive. Clearly, this was the case of a trip to Accra, Ghana. I went to be a blessing, but soon learned and received much more than I could ever give.

This had been a rather frustrating trip thus far. I was extremely glad to be along with so many of my friends, especially one of my truest friends who had been the one to open the opportunities for ministry. We had traveled over twenty-four hours to arrive in Ghana. Upon arriving, we began the tasks of carrying on a Christian Education Seminar, a Pastors' Conference, Medical Clinics, and a Mass Crusade all at the same time. There was no rest for our weary travelers.

In all the hustle it became clear that one event, the Christian Education Seminar, would have to be scratched. I was in total agreement with the need to change plans, but it made me feel a little left out since the majority of my time was to have been spent teaching in this particular seminar. Once again, I found myself wondering why I was on this assignment. I decided that the best way to discover the answer was to jump in and help in every way I could to accomplish the remaining goals of the trip. And so I did. We distributed thousands of Bibles, toys, and medical supplies to the people of Ghana, and the number of people who committed to Christ in this mostly Muslim suburb of Accra numbered in the thousands. The final few nights of our trip approached. And still I was asking, "Why am I here?"

The evening began like any other night. The local ministries were all competing to see whose ministry would receive the most credit for their participation. Of course, there were technical issues and difficulties, but the service was well under way. I had made the mistake earlier in the week of venturing into the crowd only to find myself pulled under by the masses as they reached out for prayer and hope. On this evening, I decided to stay safely on the main stage during the worship. It was quite a sight from the stage to watch the multitude of people as they swarmed the field and pressed two and three people deep by the thousands against the fences surrounding the crusade grounds.

Suddenly, a stir began in the right side of the crowd. A man leapt to his feet, took up his bed and walked around preparing to leave. We did not think it uncommon for a man to leave, but we quickly heard the rest of the story: this man had not walked in thirty-four years! Thousands of people now watched him walk around. But to me, it seemed a little staged. I know that doesn't sound like faith, but people will often fake healings just to be brought to the main stage, thus transforming the service into a show. However, as I continued to watch the crowd grow around him, I realized they were more excited than we were. The service continued, the singing resumed, and the people began to participate with a certain expectancy. Then it happened.

I had watched earlier as the people had vied for the front row seats and the standing area on the crusade grounds. This is in sharp contrast to home where so many times the middle and the back are the prime seats. Tonight, most of those who wanted to be in the front were sickly or suffered from some form of handicap that impeded their daily lives.

However, the most aggressive of those fighting for the

front were parents determined to find a cure for their child. One young daughter had entered the grounds much earlier, trailed closely by her father. Her crutches were dirty, and her feet were shriveled and contorted in a reverse position that forced her to drag them behind her. When I see someone like this, my first thoughts are always, "Oh God, could it just be her night?" Well, this night's first impressions were right. It would be her night.

The singers were in full form. Oftentimes when I am in a third world country, the music is off key and extremely loud. This evening, however, the music could not have sounded any better. Their praise seemed to usher in the presence of God. I have learned to sense His presence. I have also learned to pinpoint where His presence seems to hover during a service. I knew that to my left was a strong and heavy feeling of the tangible moving of God. So I turned to watch. It was a moment that did not need the preacher or the singers. All that was needed was simply a person in need and the only true Almighty God who delights in meeting those needs.

The area in which the little girl stood began to glow. Often, I have imagined the light of God shining down upon Paul as Christ revealed Himself on the road to Damascus. As a young boy, I remember seeing a glow of God's presence radiating around my dad as I watched him minister under the anointing of God. But this light was different. A peaceful light "overshadowed" the little girl. Perhaps this is what the Psalmist meant when he wrote of "abiding under the shadow of the Almighty". Since there is no darkness in God, then His shadow is also light.

The night seemed to pause. An altar worker knelt to the ground and motioned for the young girl to come forward. Her face was aglow and her little leg came up off the ground as she took a step forward. While the young girl's first step was still in stride, three distinct things happened. First, her crutch fell to the ground. Next, her foot straightened, and finally she planted her foot for the first time in a solid step. This process was repeated with her second foot. Each step was solid and determined. After the first few steps, the young girl's steps became quicker and quicker. I am not sure if the crowd gasped in unison or if it was just me. Tears streamed down our faces. She ran and leapt into the arms of the altar worker. From within the crowd a scream of praise erupted. The little girl beamed. Once she had no hope, but tonight she had encountered the hope of Christ. I simply dropped my head and wept as I finally realized why God had brought me here. My own faith was strengthened by this moment which I never want to forget!

Chapter 4

Mark The Time

BEING AN EAGER young pastor, I never wanted to miss an opportunity to be the first one on the scene to help one of my families in need. In my zeal to accomplish this task, I once rushed straight to the hospital in such a hurry that I had my children in tow. This was not a wise decision since my children were quite young, and the hospital room with all its sights and sounds was not the proper place for my investigative toddlers. Needless to say, this was not a successful visit. Actually, it was a horrible failure both as a parent and a pastor. As a result, this experience left me feeling a little "gun-shy" of hospital visits. Shortly after this mistake, I even made the remark that visits to the funeral home were much easier for me than the torture of hospital visitation.

It was during this fear-induced sabbatical that I received a call from one of the families of our church. They relayed the tragic news of a horrible accident that had just befallen their son. He had been working alone when suddenly a piece of equipment malfunctioned. A piece of metal flew loose and embedded itself deep into his brain. We prayed together over the telephone and I assured them we would do our best to help their family through this time. Then the church went to work preparing and delivering meals, making encouraging phone calls, and, on my part, finding someone to go to the hospital and meet with the family. Many church members and elders obliged, and, in my opinion, the family was very well supported. However, from the family's perspective, one important event had not yet occurred. Their pastor had not laid his hands on their son in prayer.

Certainly, I reasoned to myself, the prayers of the men and women who had already gone in my place would be as good as, if not better than, anything I could offer. However, this family persisted in their determination that their pastor should come to their son's bedside. So I began the long car ride

36

to the hospital in Atlanta. Of course I was a bit nervous, and it seemed my uncertainty left me awkward and vulnerable to a battle of doubt. I have found that during times of questioning my abilities and faith, God forces me to stretch in order to make me more beneficial to His Kingdom. Come to think of it, the greatest miracles I have seen have all been centered on His ability, not mine.

I arrived in the hospital waiting room. Normally in these situations, I am greeted with hugs and expressions of gratitude for making the trip, but not this time. This small framed, greatly determined mother simply grabbed my hand and said, "Let's go. It's time to pray." Quickly, she led me down the hallway to the doors that separated the main hospital from the Intensive Care Unit. While we waited to be allowed in, I silently admired the strength of character of this mother and thought how interesting it would be to see anyone try to keep *this* mom out of her son's room. Suddenly, she spun around and voiced the great concern on her heart, "Pastor, they told us the worst that could happen at this point is that he would develop pneumonia. They just notified us that he is in the first stages of pneumonia."

We walked into the room. I was accustomed to seeing tubes, pumps, and body fluids everywhere, but I was not prepared for this sight. His brain injury had affected his entire body. He was covered head to foot in a combination of bandages and bed coverings, and his body was so swollen that it was excruciating for me to even look at him. Yet, here I was to lay hands on him and pray for this man. At first, my natural inclinations led me to wonder if I should pray for his passing, but I had been brought to lay hands on him for healing. My only question: where could I place hands on him without increasing his pain?

After a thorough examination, I determined that the only place I could lay hands on him was to take hold of his big toe which was the least swollen part of his body. I felt like a fool standing there holding this man's toe, but I had come to pray, and pray we would. I began the traditional, "we thank you for the stripes of Christ and we now claim healing" prayer that pastors are expected to pray. However, somewhere in the middle of this prayer it happened. My prayer changed from an obligatory prayer to a fervent, intercessory prayer with an authority not my own.

In prayer, there are times that we ask, times we beg, and times that no matter what we say nothing changes. This time was none of the above. Asking was a part of the prayer, but an uncertain asking was out of the question. My uncertainty was replaced with a feeling that I have come to recognize ever since that day. It is a feeling that God has granted exactly what is specified. It is not a passive "whatever you desire for us" prayer. Rather it is a prayer of specified force that leaves no

38

question that God has moved. When this feeling appears, the request is given and the prayer comes quickly to an end. Without realizing what I was doing, I prayed, "Father, we ask that the doctors will actually *mark the time* that we have been praying as the time he begins to recover. Amen."

We left the room and there were no obvious changes in the man. However, there were changes in me. I had sensed a new power of authority. I had neither any clue how important this would be to me in the years to come, nor any idea as to how many people would benefit from this new revelation in my life. This mother was also changed; she had a new outlook. It was now settled within her that God would heal her son. After leaving the hospital, however, I still wondered if I would soon be called to preach his funeral.

The next morning, my phone rang at exactly 7:01. It's not unusual for a pastor's phone to ring at that time in the morning. People generally won't call before seven, so they wait until just a minute past. This morning, I wanted to ignore the ringing phone and continue sleeping about ten more minutes. However, I thought perhaps the mother was calling to say he had passed away, so I answered the phone. The mother's voice joyously reported, "They have done it, Pastor!" Confused, I asked, "They've done what?" She replied, "They have actually *marked the time* you were in the room as the time he began to recover. He is now conscious and markedly improved."

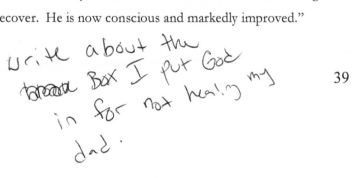
write about the ~~bread~~ Box I put God in for not healing my dad.

This I would have to see for myself. "He couldn't be that much improved," I thought to myself. I went to the ICU, but he wasn't there. I walked into the regular hospital room, and there he sat on the bed. Just a day before, he had been near death. So close, in fact, that the hospital had asked the family about the possibility of organ donation. But today God had specifically answered our prayer. Within a few days he was headed out to Bible College, planning to spend his life proclaiming what God can do in our lives when we ask believing. It is a story I never want to forget.

Now at every opportunity for prayer I silently ask God if this is one of those moments that will be marked by the miraculous.

Chapter 5

Can You Make It
To The Car?

I HAD GONE to the church early that morning to finalize the preparations for the service. Having grown up a pastor's child, I knew this was the norm for the job. On Sunday mornings, pastors tend to busily finalize those last few details that put the finishing touches on the day's plans. Our church had grown and I found this time extremely valuable, not so much for physical preparation, but for focusing upon the awesome spiritual responsibility of bringing God's message to His church.

As a rule, I generally do not answer the phone on Sunday mornings because many times it is someone who is having a bad morning trying to ensure that everyone else will also have a bad morning as well. Other times it is a worker calling to tell you they are too ill to make it to church, but of course, they are probably going to be strong enough later in the day to make it to the big sale down at the store. So, when the phone rang this morning, I hesitated; but then knowing how things had been at home lately, I decided it best that I answer. On the other end of the phone was my wife's shaking voice. Typically, her voice rings with confidence, but for some months now her voice had almost been stolen from her. It had all begun when we returned home from visiting one of our church families.

When we walked through the door of our home, things were out of place. There was mud on the floor and I was quickly blamed for it. I defended myself by pointing out that I had not even been in our muddy backyard and that my large feet leave much bigger footprints than the ones on our carpet. Suddenly, we started to notice that our house was minus a few basic items. Then the awful realization sunk in. We had been robbed.

In the final count, we lost several thousand dollars to the thief, but I would have gladly given all to him if he had left behind one priceless possession. He had stolen much more than our things. He had walked off with my wife's sense of security. He had also left behind much more than muddy shoe prints. We were left with the mark of fear which damaged our home much worse than muddy carpet.

Sometimes in life it seems you just can't get a break. Probably all we needed was a little time to process what had happened to us. Of course, we reported the robbery to the local authorities, but incredibly they only falsely accused us of perpetrating the crime ourselves. We felt helpless and frustrated without any hope of securing the identity of those who had victimized us. Finally, facing our new-found fear, we set out to try to simply recover normalcy. Little did we know we were just beginning a very long journey.

Our first child was only eight weeks old at this time and my wife was suffering from being postpartum. Now, however, we both were also suffering post-traumatic stress syndrome. Many days passed before my wife was courageous enough to venture out on her own again. One day, unfortunately, our situation worsened.

She was almost back home from running errands when she passed a van at the entrance to our road. It pulled out and began to follow her. It did not attempt in any way to be stealthy about its approach. It aggressively began to push her down the road. She passed our house trying to avoid being followed home by a strange aggressor. The van came even closer. The road ended in a cul-de-sac. The van pulled itself across the road and blocked her escape.

It was during that moment she made her decision to ram their car with as much force as possible to hopefully prevent them from being able to abduct her and our baby daughter or possibly even worse. Aggressively, she floored the car. At the last possible moment, the surprised van leapt forward off the road and out of the way. Greatly shaken, but safe, she made her way to my office at the church. Reports were filed and safety precautions were noted. However, our fear now turned to terror, and terror would rule our home for months to come.

The attacker was surprised by her aggression, but his surprise would soon turn to retaliation. An attacker must be confronted and I greatly desired to confront him. However, this attacker had the benefit of being anonymous and used it to his advantage. The next few months left us wondering what events the next day would bring. At first, it was odd things like our cars being molested in the evening. Then even stranger events occurred like the trees in our yard being chopped to pieces and trash being stolen. Later, when we were informed that money had been borrowed against our names without our knowledge, we realized the stolen garbage was for the purpose of identity theft. Finally, these bizarre events culminated with a

44

deer being disemboweled in our front yard.

In order for my wife to sleep at night, I had to keep a shotgun in my hand at first, then later by my side. For her to stay at home alone was totally out of the question. Many days during the weeks she would sit alone with our newborn in the church nursery while I worked in the office. This all occurred during a time when I was overwhelmed at work, and now my refuge, my home, brought very little solace, if any at all.

Probably the most frustrating part of it all was that I was "the pastor". I was the one whom everyone sought for answers about these types of problems. I knew exactly what to say, but my words did not result in a solution for my own home. The pressure and the tension at home became greatly magnified when we visited a pastor friend for counseling. My wife appeared to light up at his advice, which was exactly word for word what I felt that she had ignored from me. The pressures and tension at home made this a most difficult time for us.

Fear captivated her to the point that she was terrified. When one of the young men of our church ran out of gas near our house, he walked over to our home to call his parents. Not having any knowledge of these terror attacks, he began knocking on our door. This was one of those rare times when my wife was home alone. Instantly, she became terrified. She grabbed my gun and attempted to shoot through the door.

Thank God the safety on the gun would not release! She then escaped by running out through the garage. When she realized who was standing on our front porch and he realized how badly she was scared, they both broke down and wept in the driveway. Things would not improve for quite some time.

This particular Sunday morning when the phone rang at church, my wife, Christina, was at home babysitting. She felt confident enough to let me go ahead to prepare for the service. Then the call came, and when I heard her voice I knew something was wrong. "There's a German Rottweiler dog in the yard, and it doesn't seem to be going away," was her report. I must admit I was quite relieved to hear about a problem I could handle. "Do you need me to come home and deal with it?" I asked. "No," she replied, "the car is in the garage and I can get out without a problem." Quite relieved, I said, "Okay, you do that and I will deal with the dog when I get home."

After the service, I went home and scooted past the dog. Then I quickly changed and headed back outside to determine what should be done with our new yard guest. I grabbed some food. I reasoned to myself that if the dog took the food then I would let him stay in the yard because he wasn't really hurting anyone. If he didn't take the food, then he would have to be dealt with, because we definitely did not need another problem.

46

As I knelt down on the walkway, I suddenly realized that someone else had already "dealt" him a blow with buckshot to his hindquarters. Being a dog person, I began all the proper steps to reach out to this wounded animal. He responded without aggression. Actually, he responded as if he had always been around. After he ate the food, he took up residence on our front porch. It was quite a sight to see a perfect specimen of a German Rottweiler perched before our front door. He would keep guard there for over two years.

I mentioned that I am a dog person, and in our marriage the old adage holds true about opposites attracting. Yes, normally Christina did not care for animals – not just dogs, cats, or fuzzy things, but all animals. However, this animal was an exception, and Christina immediately took up with our new friend. As a matter of fact, they struck up quite a relationship, one that even I knew not to cross. Christina proudly dubbed him "Rocky", and it was clear that he tolerated me, but he "belonged" to her.

During this same period of time, our subdivision sold to a developer and surveyors began to swarm around our place. Rocky allowed them full access to our property lines and allowed them to even cross into our yard somewhat. However, whenever my wife ventured outside, Rocky would become a wall between Christina and the surveyors. Because of Christina's petite height and Rocky's great stature, he would put his head on Christina's chest and nudge her back to safety whenever he perceived anyone too close to her for his approval.

Before long, God began to open doors for me to travel and minister abroad, but I reasoned it would never work out for me to go because I couldn't leave Christina home alone. Surprisingly, my wife encouraged me to go and didn't even want anyone to stay with her while I was gone. Her response was, "If I have any problems I'll just let Rocky in the house." He seemed to be her guardian angel.

Usually when anyone pulled into our driveway, Rocky would quickly run back and forth from one side of the vehicle to the other, thus preventing anyone from getting out. Then one day we noticed that he seemed to be very selective about whom he prevented from walking up to our front door. We observed that when a brother or sister in Christ visited us, Rocky would either lovingly greet them or simply ignore them. On the other hand, when some friend or family member who was not a believer came to our house, Rocky would not let them out of their car without our permission. He became a really good meter to judge how some of our friends were doing spiritually!

People didn't always like Rocky. Some of the neighbors complained about such a big dog living in the neighborhood. My reply was simply, "I didn't bring him here and I am not going to send him away." But everyone had to admit he was one of the most perfect specimens of a German Rottweiler. And this fine fellow proudly guarded my home.

At our church one morning during a special service, our journey toward recovery was unexpectedly completed. I still vividly remember that service. The guest minister spoke about defeat and fear having us chained under the table of life, just hoping that some crumbs of happiness and blessing would fall our way. It was definitely one of the most needed and timely sermons I have ever heard.

My wife went to the altar when the preacher opened the altars for ministry. Something miraculous happened at the altar that morning. Christina was finally able to release, or find release from, the fear that had gripped her for over two years!

After the service, I received another telephone call from Christina. She had just arrived home and called to deliver the astounding news, "Rocky is nowhere to be found!" Immediately, I drove home and searched for him, but there was no sign of Rocky. To this day, there still has been no sign of Rocky. For over two years, he faithfully guarded the door of our home. Then, on the very morning my wife was set free from the bondage of fear, we had unknowingly told Rocky goodbye for the last time. He had done a great job. Our home was safe. My wife was healed. We would never forget.

Chapter 6

Tears Of Joy

SOME EXPERIENCES IN our lives are merely momentary distractions that seem to hinder us from making progress. Other experiences become beneficial occurrences which actually promote the course we have set for our lives. These experiences are encapsulated, as all our lives are, in those increments of time that begin fresh with each new day. Some days we fondly remember and others we plead to forget. Yet only a few days become a marker for the rest of our lives. So it was for me during three days of my sixth grade school year.

Our church was still relatively small, and everyone knew everyone very well. It was not today's streamlined approach to church. There was still time set aside when the congregation shared their prayer requests and praise reports. For many weeks, the prayer requests for one little boy burdened the hearts of this congregation, and the people had prayed fervently for his physical healing from disease. Today, the congregation was anxiously awaiting a praise report. But it would not come today. Instead, the news was what the church had prayed against. This little fellow was being sent home from the hospital with no hope. His life expectancy: only three days.

The tension was thick. Everyone had believed and prayed for a miracle, but today reality had set in. It seemed too late now for that miracle. Three days would be just enough time to make all the funeral preparations. Three days meant people would plan on attending a funeral probably the next weekend. In just three days, his memorial service would be finalized and the long wait for a miracle would be over.

In times like these, everyone looks to the pastor. He is supposed to know the right thing to say to make everyone feel better and press on through tragedy. As a pastor, I personally have found that during times like these, I am praying not to outwardly break down myself, while inwardly pleading for God's guidance. On this day, however, I was not the one to whom everyone turned. Standing up at the front of the church stood my pastor, my dad.

Knowing now after years of pastoring what I didn't know then as a boy, I can only imagine what must have been going on inside of Dad's mind and spirit at that moment. The words he was about to utter would make or break his ministry in the eyes of these people. A pastor is judged, sometimes harshly, for every word he utters.

Dad began to speak. I don't remember if it was with boldness or not, but what he said was certainly as bold as "Lazarus, come forth!" Dad stood in front of all these hurting, bewildered people and proclaimed, "I have heard from God. If we fast and pray for three days, this child will be healed on the third day." It definitely did not seem like the right thing to say. Instantly, critics began murmuring in their thoughts, "You should not get their hopes up; don't you know you can't back that up?" But God had spoken, and Dad was determined to lead his congregation to obey God. A group of men followed his lead and signed up to fast for the next three days. I was the youngest to join their number.

The wait was on. The next three days were grueling for all involved. The young boy's family struggled to grasp onto hope, yet they prepared to say goodbye. Dad's critics were anxious to prove him wrong. The men who were fasting were not considered spiritual giants in the community. People probably would not have picked us, but we felt chosen by God. Our number was made up of construction and factory workers, their bold, young pastor who was my dad, and me, his twelve-year-old son. One of the men in our group was also in need of healing himself since he was scheduled for surgery the following week to unclog his tear ducts. We all sensed that God was about to do something miraculous.

We faithfully fasted and prayed with God's help. Then the time came. The men were called, and together we went and gathered around the young boy at home on his death bed. We began to pray. There was no bright and shining light, neither peals of thunder across the sky, nor any audible voice of God, but the presence of God filled his room and we all knew that something had transpired. In fact, this presence of God was so heavy that everyone in the room began to weep. Even the man among us who had been physically unable to cry for several months now had tears streaming from his eyes!

When the prayer ended, doubt had been washed away by tears of joy. God had visited the room and there was no doubt that all were changed. Not only was the man visibly healed from the clogged tear ducts, but everyone in the room was well. The young boy on his death bed was miraculously healed, just as God had spoken this promise to Dad! Immediately, this young fellow's coloring improved significantly and he rapidly began to regain strength. Within a short period of time, he was a completely normal little boy and the doctor's tests miraculously could no longer detect any sign of the disease.

There once had been a death sentence of three days, but now the days ahead held a bright new future with a clean bill of health. Three days have since turned into many years, but it was a visit from God that I will never forget.

Chapter 7

I Have Fought
The Good Fight

I CLEARLY REMEMBER the weeks leading up to September eighth that year. I knew Dad had been laid off from work and was considering a new job. At my young age, however, I didn't realize that we would have to move for Dad to take his new job. That September morning was one every little fellow looks forward to. It was my sixth birthday. My parents gave me my presents first, and then it was off to school. I thought it strange that I did not have to wait until after school to receive my presents, but I didn't complain.

During school there was a small party for me. Afterwards, my parents came early to pick me up. My teacher told me good-bye, and I left planning to see her the next day. As we left school, my first glimpse of our family truck revealed the shocking truth to me. In the back of our truck were my birthday gifts along with the majority of everything we owned. That was when I first realized we were moving.

No change has ever been as traumatic as my sixth birthday, but even today I still feel very apprehensive as my birthday approaches because it has often been a day of major change in my life. For the last several years, I have chosen to spend my birthdays abroad in foreign lands. That way they seem to pass quietly without notice. All in all, these changes usually have made a positive impact on my life, as was the case on my sixth birthday.

We drove from our little country town to the outskirts of Atlanta where our new home was located at our denominational headquarters. Within the denomination, these headquarters were affectionately called "The Campground". Here my dreams would blossom, my calling would come, and I would meet people who would later become some of the dearest friends of my life. It really was a great place to live for a young boy. To my delight there were ball fields, tennis courts, go-kart tracks, a gymnasium, a playground, two Olympic-sized swimming pools and woods for exploring. Yet best of all, the residents were retired pastors and their wives. As a young man with the calling of God on my life, there could not have been a better place to grow up.

My parents would host in our home these men and women of faith who had blazed the trail taking the Gospel into the North Georgia area. I wandered freely from house to house where I was pampered by many sets of adoptive grandparents. I was treated to cakes, cookies, candies, and, best of all, stories. I eagerly listened to their stories of the miracles of God.

To this day, these stories still encourage me in my walk of faith. Because I was privileged to hear them first hand, these stories seemed all the more real to me. Some of these stories provided inspiration, and others pointed me toward wisdom by learning how to avoid the mistakes of others. As a young boy, I received encouragement and instruction, but most of all, I gained a respect and love for those who are seasoned in the things of God. After becoming a young pastor myself, I cherished even more deeply those who had walked before me and their stories of faith. Their stories I still love to retell even today.

Time passed and I became a young pastor myself. One day while in seminary, I arrived uncharacteristically late to class and there was only one empty seat left in the classroom. As a result of that chance meeting, the young man seated next to me later became a part of our church staff and a pastor that I greatly admire. I am so grateful that was the only seat available. From that night forward, our friendship steadily grew. About a year later he joined our staff, and he and his wife and entire family became part of our extended family.

After working together for some time, we took a short drive one day over the mountains to Ellijay, Georgia, to visit his grandfather. He was outside cutting firewood when we arrived. At this first meeting, my spirit immediately sensed that I was in the presence of a true man of God. He was a retired pastor who had spent his life bringing the Gospel to the hills of North Georgia. Instantly, I was at ease and looked forward to hearing his stories and gleaning wisdom from the experiences of this pioneer of the faith. I was privileged to visit him again many times, and at every encounter I would take away some blessing and always look forward to our next visit.

We did not know our relationship with this great man of God would soon be cut short because of his cancer diagnosis. We prayed and sought God for healing, but healing did not come. I began to truly cherish every moment spent with him. Then one day the dreaded call came, and we began our last trip over the mountain to visit him. We were told he had not eaten in several days, and if we were to visit with him at all, it needed to be soon.

There is a somber mood that settles over a home when someone is about to pass over. Everyone wants to keep their loved one comfortable during their final moments on earth and not allow any disturbances. Such was the setting when we entered their home this day. His wife kept a constant eye toward the living room where he lay in a hospital bed. We were told he was unresponsive, and we were advised not to expect much more from him.

As we approached his bed, I wondered how many times through the years his old body had been responsive to the presence of God. How many times had he laid hands on the sick to feel God's power surge through him? How many times had he felt the power of God run up and down his spine while he was preaching? In my mind, I silently recalled the stories he had told me of times he was overcome by God's presence while driving and arrived at his next destination unaware of how he made it there.

Suddenly a heavy presence of God settled into the room. I wondered if he was about to pass over to the other side. It felt like heaven was about to open. Then his eyes sprung open and he sat straight up in the bed and reached out, grabbing us both by the arm. He looked us both straight in the eye, and with the voice of a mighty prophet he declared,

> *"I have fought a good fight.*
> *I have finished my course.*
> *I have kept the faith."*

Boldly, he commissioned us to do the same and then settled back down into his final rest. We stood there shocked for a moment. Then in silent awe of the presence of God, we both realized that, just as Elijah had passed his mantle to Elisha, so this man of God had passed *his* mantle of anointing to *us*. The torch had been passed. It was now ours to carry. The chance to blaze new trails was now up to us. He had faithfully completed his work on earth and commissioned us to carry on the faith!

I am certain he is now in the great cloud of witnesses that are in the presence of our Heavenly Father cheering us on to finish the course that is set before us. It was certainly a moment in time I will never forget.

Chapter 8

Lord, Do I Have To?

I HAVE COME to the conclusion that some people disagree for the simple pleasure of disagreeing. I am not sure if they consciously realize they actually enjoy it, or if it's just second nature for them to be disagreeable. I have also learned that when people continue arguing about a topic at extended lengths, they are either unsure of the truth or don't want to apply this truth in their own lives. Because of such disagreements, factions of people who believe a certain way have joined together and formed their own little group. Thus denominations are born.

I suppose being raised in one of those factions of faith I have certain programmed responses to questions of doctrine, but I have learned to question myself and my training when it does not line up with what is clearly outlined in Scripture. There are certain teachings I received from my parents and church that I see as very beneficial to a healthy life, but I cannot prove them from Scripture so I must relegate them to practical suggestions and not divine commands. One foundation of my faith, however, is clearly outlined in Scripture. I find it very difficult for anyone to conceivably deny the presence and activity of the Holy Spirit in the daily life of every believer.

I would not say that I am a Pentecostal, *per se*, because they seem to stress the baptism of the Holy Spirit above everything else. In contrast, I am determined that my life will be spent stressing the importance of salvation above all else. Charismatic would not be a good description of my worship style either, because I am neither extremely flamboyant in style, nor do I believe the gifts of the Spirit are at the discretion of the believer, but are rather measured and used at the Spirit's directive. Spirit-led would probably be the most accurate description that I would choose to align myself with. With all that said, I plainly believe and encourage the believer to experience the baptism of the Holy Spirit.

However, there was a time in my life when I would not have encouraged this view. It wasn't because I doubted the experience, but I had become cynical from being personally damaged by those who abused the experience. Some of the greatest deliverances and radical changes in the lives of people occur within churches that stress the baptism of the Holy Spirit. On the other hand, there is usually an undercurrent of people in these churches who like to "dabble" in the supernatural. This abuse is what detests me.

As a pastor, I have found that those who stress the gifts of the Spirit are more likely to suddenly "feel led of the Spirit" to skip out on any form of commitment. As a Christian school principal, my experience is that non-Pentecostal parents have paid their bills better than Pentecostals about ten to one. In fact, even non-Christian parents have paid their kids' tuition better than the majority of Pentecostals who have attended our school. We have thousands of dollars of outstanding tuition from people who claimed, "God told them they no longer needed to pay what they owed." While people from the more traditional denominations have lied to me or about me behind my back, the Pentecostals and Charismatics have done it to my face with a smile. So, obviously, I began to question the experience of the baptism of the Holy Spirit because almost everyone I knew who stressed the "Pentecostal" experience displayed few other evidences of a Christian life.

It was at this point in my life when I found myself heading up a team of people to travel to Haiti for a Crusade which would include drama outreach and a Pastors' Training Seminar. We had been a part of this seminar for several years, and I always looked forward to the opportunity of helping train the local pastors. Since the program was an ongoing ministry with several guest pastors participating, our topics were assigned to us ahead of time. My topic arrived several weeks in advance of my departure, and I was not very happy when I received the assignment of teaching on "The Baptism of the Holy Spirit".

This trip was exciting to me because I was leading a team of people most of whom had never traveled outside the United States. This week would launch some of my team into international ministry, while others would decide never to leave the States again. As for me, I was having one of the most discouraging weeks I had experienced in a long time. The Crusade was minimal in its success. The street drama outreach was a blessing for those involved, but I was never able to go with them because I was teaching the Pastors' Training Seminar.

It was the conclusion of my final day teaching the series on the baptism of the Holy Spirit. Before I handed the podium over to our local missionary, I looked out across the faces of those whom I had been teaching all week and recognized a questioning look on all of them. Although I was struggling personally, I was instantly determined not to be struggling professionally. Without giving it much thought, I looked out at the students and said, "Okay, you have heard about it. Now who wants it?" The interpreter looked surprised but translated the statement nonetheless. Instantly, many lined up to receive what was offered. The problem was that I did not know if I really had anything to offer them. I instructed them that the only way they would be receiving this gift was by the example from Scripture when the apostles laid their hands on the people and they received the Holy Spirit. So that's what we did.

Many of the students began to shake while others did nothing. Some even spoke with other tongues. During this entire time, I thought to myself, "Well, I have seen all of this before." Then a blind man heard all the commotion and stumbled in off the streets. When he stumbled back out the door just as blind as when he came in, I wondered to myself, "When will I truly see the move of the Holy Spirit?" The line had dispersed and people were rejoicing, when even more cynical than before I said, "Is there anyone else?"

He and his young apprentice had sat stoically in the back of the room during the entire lecture series and this impromptu altar service. It was obvious the elder statesman, a pastor of a more traditional church, did not approve or believe in the modern working of the Holy Spirit. It would not have shocked me if they simply walked out the door. However, much to my surprise, they both stood and stepped out into the aisle and came to the front and stood before me. Through the interpreter, I asked if the younger pastor wanted to receive the Holy Spirit. He replied, "*oui*", so I reached to lay my hands on his head. Because he was a very tall young man, I thought it was going to be a little difficult to accomplish this task. As my hand approached his forehead, it was as if lightning shot from my hand into his body. He screamed and began to jump around as the Holy Spirit manifested in his life. I remember thinking, "I have even seen that before."

After the commotion settled a bit, the elder pastor walked up and stood before me. I asked through the interpreter if he desired the Holy Spirit and he indicated affirmatively, so I laid my hands on him. There was no electric shock this time, just a strong presence of God. I leaned in and began to pray. He began to pray in tongues as the Holy Spirit filled his life. I remember thinking that the tongues that were manifesting were a miracle because of his strong disapproval of the topic as I had taught it. Then I realized something else. Not only was he speaking in tongues, but I understood every word. Not only me, but everyone who spoke English understood exactly what he was saying. For several minutes, he continued to declare the Glory of Jehovah God in perfect English.

At first, my level of faith plunged as I thought to myself, "Certainly this man must have traveled to the States or have studied English." Curiously, I asked the interpreter to find out how much English the man knew. He reported that the man knew no more English than the word "hello". Profoundly amazed, I became greatly humbled. Although I had previously heard people speak in tongues or shout and scream, today I witnessed what occurred on the day of Pentecost. God had been glorified through a gift that enabled all who were around to hear the truth that was being proclaimed.

I still encounter what I call "flakes" of the spirit-filled movement, people who want the gifts but don't want to live a life that glorifies the Giver of the gifts. However, I no longer doubt the experience. I have seen God fill His people over and over again with the power to be His witnesses. Like the apostle of old, "I would that you all spoke with other tongues." As for me, I am determined never to forget how God restored my faith.

Chapter 9

Daddy, I'm Thirsty

S OMETIMES WE FORGET that our doctors are merely human. We tend to believe the misconception that somehow they know everything. However, it has been my observation that most of the time our bodies speak for themselves, and a good doctor simply reads the signs and symptoms which point in the direction of healing. Perhaps today's doctors aren't permitted the time to observe and study their patient's underlying symptoms because of their requirements to quickly diagnose a large number of patients. After dealing with patients who abuse the system, maybe some doctors simply become prejudiced and callused and look no further than the major signs of illness. For whatever reasons, sometimes doctors simply make a wrong diagnosis.

Living in a small rural town, I was blessed to have a very wise doctor who was never too busy to listen to all my complaints and symptoms. He was very gifted in discerning the root causes of these signs. However, as new parents one of our first requirements was to select a pediatrician. After being accustomed to the excellent relationship I enjoyed with our family doctor, it was quite a challenge to develop a similar relationship with multiple pediatricians within a large practice.

Our first child, Bethany, had recently turned two years old when my wife began noticing some very odd symptoms. The most confusing part was that the symptoms were intermittent. As young parents experiencing these new stages of development for the first time, we thought perhaps this was just a phase of the "terrific twos". However, during the next week my wife became convinced there was something medically wrong, so she took Bethany to the pediatrician. Since it was the beginning of the flu season, she was diagnosed with the flu and was expected to improve within a few days.

Over the next thirty-six hours, our daughter's health steadily declined. Christina was certain there was something seriously wrong. She called the pediatrician to seek further advice and was given the last appointment of the day. When they arrived, Bethany was examined by another pediatrician in the practice.

This time, my wife requested a simple test to determine if our child was having kidney problems similar to those her mother experienced at the same age. This request was quickly dismissed by the doctor as irrelevant. Christina was extremely frustrated that she had been repeatedly and rudely told that our daughter had the flu. As our daughter's advocate, my wife made one final appeal for some type of testing, but the doctor emphatically refused to even discuss it. In hindsight, we should have demanded the test because it would have revealed the truth about this pediatrician's false diagnosis of the so-called "flu" our daughter was experiencing.

As the weekend approached, Bethany became extremely lethargic. Saturday morning, Christina called the doctor yet again to plead her case. The doctor remained just as aloof in her response as before. With the doctor offering no advice as to why our little girl was constantly thirsty and almost comatose, my wife phoned me with her condition to alert me that we needed to seek immediate medical care for her.

It was a few weeks before Christmas and I was out buying Bethany's first "big" bed for a present. I had just recently invested in my first cell phone, and that day it was worth its weight in gold because my wife urgently needed me since our daughter desperately needed help. Christina was obviously very upset not only with the doctor's uncaring attitude, but primarily with Bethany's rapidly declining health. Extremely concerned, I quickly returned home and immediately we left for the hospital. As a young pastor's family, we had no insurance, no money, and had never faced anything like this before.

Less than a mile from home, our daughter began to plead for something to drink. I stopped and purchased her a soft drink and then continued toward the hospital. I had no clue that my answer to her pleas was actually poisoning her further. Every good father wants to meet not only their children's needs, but also their wants. However, I painfully learned on this day that sometimes when I am pleading to God for something, He may be withholding it, not out of indifference, but for my own good.

After an hour drive, we arrived at what we considered the best children's hospital in Atlanta. When we entered the emergency room that Saturday, we were shocked that the waiting room resembled a "war zone".

74

There were people waiting everywhere. Babies were screaming, toddlers were scurrying about, and parents were obviously irritated. Since it was the height of the soccer season, there were kids everywhere wearing different color jerseys holding ice packs on their injured shoulders, legs, or heads. Over in the corner, I observed one Hispanic couple clutching their first little newborn with a look of terror on their face because, from what I could perceive, the baby had its first low grade fever.

As we approached the triage area, we suddenly realized why the chaos was so prevalent. The hospital was greatly understaffed on that Saturday. There was only one, lonely, little nurse who appeared to be suffering from "battle fatigue" in this war zone. After a quick glance at our daughter, we were instructed to sign in and then were sent to the far side of the waiting room. From the looks of the parents around us, our wait would be a long one. There were many who had already waited through the chaos for so long that they were now adding to the turmoil with their obvious irritation. I watched as parent after parent verbally accosted the nurse to no avail.

Amidst all this turmoil, I sat down and began to pray over my little girl. She was lifeless in my arms. I remember thinking, "Please, someone look past the bumps and scrapes and see that my little girl is very ill." Normally, I am a very forceful person, but today I was defeated and just sat quietly

75

praying. All of a sudden, I heard that familiar voice of the Holy Spirit as He said to me, "Stop the nurse and tell her she is doing a good job." "But Lord," I replied, "she is not doing a good job." Over my objections, the Lord strongly reiterated His prompting to me, *"Stop her and tell her she is doing a good job!"*

As I approached that small-framed little nurse, I think she probably braced herself for a blasting from this big, monstrous man. I gently looked down into her weary face and said, "I don't care what anyone else says; I think you are doing a good job." She blankly stared at me and waited to see if I was finished, then turned abruptly and marched off. I remember thinking sarcastically, "A lot of good that did, God!" As I watched her walk past the entire line of patients and around the corner, I wondered what would happen next. Since that time, I have given it much thought, and all that I have ever been able to discern is that she must have moved my daughter's chart from the bottom to the top. She calmly appeared back around the corner. With a smirk on her face as she passed all of those who had been screaming at her, she walked directly up to me and said, "Bring her and come with me."

We were ushered into a small room first, but then we were immediately led into an examination room. Suddenly, the room was filled with an emergency medical team of doctors who quickly surrounded her and began working feverishly while we watched helplessly but prayed continually. It would be some time later before they could take time to explain to us the seriousness of our daughter's condition.

We later learned that her blood sugar at the time of our arrival was 777. Medically speaking, she was in diabetic ketoacidosis which meant that her body was filled with poison. The doctors told us that she would be an insulin dependent diabetic for life. Indelibly etched in my memory from those first few moments when the doctors rushed in to save our young daughter's life, is this statement one of them somberly declared to us, "If this child had not made it here right this moment, she would be dead."

I know now that my daughter was truly dying in my arms in that waiting room. In just another moment, she would have been gone. I also know that I will never forget that God still speaks today, and for those who listen, there truly is life.

Chapter 10

I Want To Buy A Cow

I AM CALLED TO AMERICA. That was my theme as a young minister. I never really understood why anyone would want to travel outside the country to preach the Gospel when there were so many opportunities to minister right here at home. You see, I did not understand the call to the nations. Many people ask me today, and many of them quite pragmatically, "Why do you travel when there are lost people here?" My answer is that it is not by my choice. My plans were to support others on their way. My parents had taught me the biblical principle of sowing into the mission field, and thus I was content in sending others. Then the Lord spoke to me and told me to get prepared because I would be leaving the country.

I did not know where I would be going. I had always respectfully declined invitations from missionaries to visit them in the field. Even after the Lord spoke this into my heart, I continued to reject offers to visit the mission field. Through a series of strange events, one night a young Cajun missionary invited me to Haiti to teach part of a training seminar for pastors. I instantly knew that I was to go.

Since that time, I have traveled the world preaching the Gospel of my Lord Jesus Christ. I can't say it is my desire to go, but I definitely understand the call to go. Three things always happen on these trips. First and foremost, the Gospel changes lives. Secondly, the experience changes my life. Last, but not least, the fresh revelations from God changes the life of our church. Actually, there is one other thing that always happens. I am absolutely exhausted when I return home.

I hate to fly. People tell me it's because I haven't flown enough. If that is the case, I wonder when I will start liking it since I already average between fifteen to twenty flights per year. Many times I have traveled with just one or two companions, while other times I have been part of large teams. It doesn't matter to me if there are several people traveling in our group or just a few, I still am one of those people who want all the plans set, settled, and charted far in advance.

Such was the case recently when my staff was busily planning a ministry team trip to Honduras. Quite unexpectedly, we were approached by a businessman of our church who wanted to "buy a cow for someone". This was quite an unusual request. In fact, it was an extremely unique situation that we had never faced before. Undaunted, however, we quickly began to secure the purchase of the livestock in a foreign land, which was no easy task.

The next task at hand was to decide who would receive the blessing of this cow. You see, if someone walked up to us in America and gave us a cow, it would probably be quite a nuisance for most of us. However, in the mountains of Honduras, giving someone a dairy cow was like handing them the ticket to a bright future with a prosperous new career.

We first considered the local pastor up in the mountains. Not that we thought he was sitting around praying for a cow, but if we wanted to bless someone, it seemed only logical to choose the man of God who had been faithful to spread the Gospel. However, God soon clearly showed us His choice in the matter. During a phone conversation discussing other details about the plans for our trip with our missionary in Honduras, he unexpectedly shared this story of how a stranger had blessed him during his recent ministry.

God gave this missionary a very compassionate heart and it was not unusual for him to give away everything he had. He had recently found himself in just that situation which we knew to be quite common for him: he had given away all of his supply money to others who had greater needs than he. Nonetheless, he had packed his last supplies and began a ministry trip up into the mountains accompanied by an aide.

After several days, the missionary and his companion had totally exhausted their supply of food. During their travel, they happened upon a humble family who lived relatively close to a local church in the mountains. The husband of this family was the groundskeeper for the church. He worked hard to keep the church grounds looking very nice and watched over the church to protect everything from being stolen from the building. When the groundskeeper recognized these men's need for food, he invited these strangers into his home. His family prepared the last of *their* beans and fed them to our missionary and his companion. When I heard this story, I knew our search for someone to bless had come to an end, because this groundskeeper had sown a harvest that would soon bring him a reward he never expected.

After our arrival in Honduras, we traveled up the mountain and arrived safely in the village. There, waiting for us when we arrived, was the beautiful cow and her calf that we had purchased. In preparation for ministry that night, we moved the cow and her calf off to the side and proceeded further up the hill to set up our equipment to present the Gospel of Christ on a big movie screen. The population of this small village was no more than two hundred, but that evening the town swelled to over 1,500 people who were attracted by the sight of the foreigners and the big movie screen. Our team blessed the children with candy and balloons while the crowd gathered.

We were ready to present the Gospel, but before we began, one of our team members and I walked to the front of the crowd. We called out the man's name and asked him and his family to come to the front. The surprised family then stood up in front of one of the largest gatherings this little town had ever seen. They had no clue why they were being called to the front. I shared the story from Scripture of the little widow and her empty barrel of grain. I told them about how she had honored God by blessing the man of God and how this act had brought provision for the entire family. I asked the man if he remembered this story. He affirmed that he did. Then I reminded him of when he had done the same with our missionary. He very humbly dropped his head and acknowledged it was true.

I removed from my pocket a large piece of paper and asked him if he knew the name that was written on the document. He replied that it was indeed his name. I explained to him this paper was his deed to the dairy cow and her calf which were given as a blessing to him. He simply stood still in silent shock as the dairy cow and her calf were brought to the front. Can you imagine the feeling of realizing your life will never be the same again? For Americans, it might compare to the realization of your increased status in life if Ed McMan unexpectedly appeared at your door with a giant check! After somewhat recovering from the initial shock of this unexpected attention, we were able to hand him the reins to his new future.

Since then, we have received reports that the life of this family has been radically changed. They were about to be forced to leave town in search of work. Instead, his family is now fed by the milk from this dairy cow and the excess milk is sold to meet other needs. Thus, a whole new life of blessings has been opened up to them. All of this happened because he was willing to give his best to the children of God. Let us never forget that those who lend unto the least of these lend unto God, and God always repays.

Chapter 11

You Can Go
"HOME" Now

T HE DAY STARTED like most every day I spend abroad when traveling to remote areas to reach out to the local people and proclaim the Gospel of Jesus Christ. Regardless of my careful planning, my travel schedules are best summarized by the phrase "hurry-up and wait". This particular day, the schedule required more than the usual amount of patience. Finally, we arrived in one of the poorest shanty towns in all of Honduras. We began to set up a large screen and projector as the local people curiously began to gather around. Our ministry team dressed as clowns and gave candy to the children while we prepared to start the movie. Everything was proceeding as planned until the first of many rain showers arrived overhead shortly after the movie started.

We covered the equipment as best we could and hoped that the rain would soon stop. We continued the movie, and most of the crowd stayed and braved the downpours. The rain persisted for quite some time, and finally we simply surrendered to the elements and gave up. However, after we shut off the film, many in the crowd continued to stand and wait. Instantly, God triggered my memory and reminded me of a similar situation in Africa some years before.

The crowd in Ghana, Africa, still numbered in the thousands after the service came to an end. One of my dearest friends was leading the crowd in the prayer of salvation when, all of a sudden, the bottom fell out of the sky and torrential rains began to pound down upon all. I remember thinking to myself, "Well, that's just like the enemy." Then I looked around in amazement and realized that of the two thousand people standing at the altar, not one was leaving. I thought how at home many people use the excuse of rain sprinkles to justify staying home from church services. In stark contrast, the people here stood on a ball field in an open air campaign in torrential rain and waited until they received what they had come after.

Inspired by this scene, I steadfastly purposed to myself, "If they are staying, then I am staying." Two thousand souls stood that day as the rain washed the dust from their faces and the blood of Christ washed the sins from their heart! When the prayer was over, we proclaimed them baptized in the name of the Father, the Son, and the Holy Ghost. We all went away physically soaked by the rain, yet spiritually encouraged that God had also "rained" down and met with those who called upon His name.

So here I was again. This time, however, the people standing before me did not number into the thousands. Nonetheless, each of the thirty souls standing in the rain today was just as important to Christ. They determinedly stood there waiting to identify with their Creator and enter into a personal relationship with Him. Through watching just a brief glimpse of the movie and seeing the expressions of the love of Christ demonstrated toward their children by the missionaries, they had decided to choose Christ. That's exactly what we did. I led them in the prayer of salvation. They repeated the prayer, and Christ completed the work. Those who had no "home" now have a Home in Heaven. They smiled and I was humbled, and then we all ran for cover from the rain.

Chapter 12

Like Fire In My Bones

S OME PEOPLE CHOOSE to learn only by experiencing things for themselves, yet this may not always be the wisest path to choose. On the other hand, most people try to teach others by sharing their experiences. All of us have heard wise, mature people genuinely plead their case with the younger generation when they say, "I just don't want you to make the same mistakes I did." However, instead of heeding this wise advice, most people still stubbornly continue on their own path repeating those same mistakes and oftentimes making many others as well. In my life, on occasion I have been extremely grateful when I have heeded someone's advice warning me to avoid certain dangers, while other times I have been sorely disappointed after following the advice of others to venture out and try some new experience like dining at their recommended restaurant. Therefore, I think that one of the most delicate situations in life is learning when to yield to someone else's life lessons.

I remember one such life lesson which I learned through my own experience when I was a young evangelist preaching in a small church in my hometown. The evening had been a tremendous success in my mind. I was so excited because my sermon actually seemed to make sense this time. The altars were filled with people and others were rejoicing throughout the church. Since I was in the midst of a Pentecostal church where there was loud rejoicing going on, I decided to join in.

Overflowing with feelings of victory, I expressed myself the same way that a prize fighter does when he pulls his arm to his chest, makes a fist, and then quickly thrusts it up into the air. However, as I carried out my intended actions, what actually happened was that as my fist was proceeding skyward, the pastor of that church simultaneously leaned in towards me to tell me something that I am sure would have been extremely spiritual. However, as he unexpectedly leaned forward while I was expressing my joy, my fist made powerful contact with his lower jaw in an amazing upper cut.

He fell back and suddenly the rejoicing was silenced all over the church. Shocked, I thought to myself, "I have just killed the Pastor." Thank God I was wrong about his prognosis. However, he did suffer a total blackout from my knock-out punch, and was revived with visions of stars around his head. On that note, the service quickly came to a close. Needless to say, I never preached for that pastor again. However, I did learn a valuable lesson of self-control from my experience that I will never forget.

Another lesson that has greatly impacted my life was not a lesson that I personally experienced, but rather a lesson shared with me as a boy from the vast personal experiences of a retired pastor. He told me of an exciting service where he was preaching and the power of God was so strong that he suddenly had the urge to run. Anyone who remembers the old architectural style of churches in America may remember the small banister or "fence" that typically separated the raised platform at the front of the church from the rows of pews. When the urge to run came over this pastor, there was no way to quickly go around the banister, so he decided to hurdle it. He recounted to me, "It was *like fire in my bones;* I had to go!"

At the peak of a perfect high hurdle over the banister, he suddenly remembered that a cable had been strung across the room in preparation for the Christmas play. However, that realization occurred much too late for this tall preacher to change his course. Suddenly, he was "clotheslined" by the invisible cable and headed quickly back to earth in the opposite direction. He landed with a resounding thud back on the platform flat on his back. Obviously, his message had come to an end, but an important life lesson had been learned the hard way.

Upon hearing this story as a young boy, I decided this was a life lesson I should learn from the experiences of others. This life lesson has never left me and is one I still remember: one should always look before they leap.

Chapter 13

I Need To Ask You
One More Time

WHEN I WAS in the sixth grade, I was running outside and tripped over some wire, fell and broke my arm. I really don't remember exactly how that happened. One minute I was running full speed chasing after my dog, and the next thing I remember is collapsing into my mother's arms with a broken arm. I was put into a splint and then we went on to church. I was to be seen the next day by the doctor for an official cast.

After being examined by the doctor the following day, he explained to us that it was necessary to have my arm set in the direction opposite of the break. This meant I would have to endure the pain again while my arm was broken in the other direction. I was obviously uncomfortable about this news. However, most of my discomfort was not from what I knew was about to happen, but rather from the fact that my dad was in the room. At twelve years old, I did not want to cry in front of Dad. He had never said anything to make me feel that way, but because of my great admiration for him, I just wanted my dad to be proud of me. I remember this as one of the proudest days of my life because I did not cry in front of Dad.

Dad was always able to handle anything. Dad was never broke and always had a plan. He could fix it if it was broken or build it if we needed it. Dad did not have a regular job. Occasionally, he would partner in a business venture or build a house to sale. However, my dad was, first and foremost, a pastor. Dad was not a pastor who did it merely as a job, but the pastor who represented the Most High God in the community.

My dad told me many marvelous stories of the sovereignty of Almighty God which increased my faith. God protected Dad when people threatened him with guns, and sometimes God revealed to my dad someone who would live even when their doctors had told them there was no hope.

God's choice was always the outcome. One story, however, has always stood out to me above all the rest.

One day, Dad was in the middle of a business transaction with a friend who had secured the services of a local businessman to draw up the necessary paperwork for them. They had been talking for a while when God prompted my dad to ask this businessman a question. Dad quickly obeyed God and stopped in the middle of business and said to the man, "Do you mind if I ask if you are ready to meet God?" The man quickly replied, "Oh, yes, Pastor, I was saved and baptized when I was a little boy." Assuming everything was fine, Dad continued with business until he felt that same pricking at his heart again.

Imagine the war going on inside of Dad as he was sitting there. This man was doing him a tremendous favor, and he was about to really upset him. "Sir," Dad interrupted again, "I just feel like *I need to ask you one more time*. Are you sure you are ready to meet God?" With a little bit of irritation the man replied, "Yes, I told you I am saved."

As the meeting was concluding, the prompting from God came to Dad once again. Obediently, Dad looked at this man and said, "God just told me to tell you that you could be sitting here today eat up with cancer, and you need to make sure that you are ready to meet Him."

Three weeks later the call came. The gentleman was in a hospital dying of cancer and he wanted Dad to come. When Dad walked into his hospital room this gentleman confessed, "Preacher, you tried to warn me and I just would not listen." Dad prayed with the man as he returned to the Lord and surrendered his life to God.

Within six weeks he passed away, but when he left here he was truly ready to meet God. Dad preached his funeral, not because he was his pastor, but because he was willing to obey God. Never forget that you might be the last person to obey the prompting of the Holy Spirit to share the Gospel with those you encounter.

Chapter 14

Reluctant Miracles

SOME NIGHTS ARE harder than others. We usually think our weariness is either the result of physical exhaustion from the events of the day or the remnant of a poor night's rest from the previous evening. Far too often, however, we forget that some nights are hard simply because that is the plan of the enemy. Scripture teaches us that our battles are not against "flesh and blood", but rather against those forces of the evil kingdom of this world.

This was one of those nights. We were ministering in the community of Borel, which is about a two hour drive from Port-au-Prince, Haiti. During the days, we had been teaching a seminar on the topic of "The Believer's Authority". We had emphatically and repeatedly stressed to these local pastors and church leaders that we are given **authority in the name of Jesus** over every demonic force. This evening, the validity of this teaching would be challenged as we bore the brunt of the enemy's anger over this truth being proclaimed in "his town".

Since there is not much to do in a small jungle town in the evening, the sight of foreigners usually attracts a large crowd for an evening service. Thus, we found it extremely odd to find the church almost empty. Finally, a small crowd filled the room and the service began. After some attempts at singing, some long prayers, and a few testimonies, it was time for my friend to preach. The electrical power suddenly shut off and the room became totally dark as soon as the preaching began.

Being almost totally exhausted, I was tempted with the thought that perhaps this was a good sign to get some rest. However, it was clearly evident this was an attack from the enemy, and I knew that I must persevere and not let him win this battle. With renewed determination, I retrieved my flashlight and converted it into a small lantern. Thus, by the light of my makeshift lantern, the preaching continued.

I noticed people were moving around outside. However, they were not coming into the church. Sensing something was wrong, I began to pray for the evening. Almost immediately, the missionary leaned over and shared with me the situation. He explained, "The people are afraid to come into the room because some of the students want to test if what you have been preaching is true or not." Realizing that I still did not understand, the missionary continued, "They have gone to the local voodoo temple and brought a demon possessed girl to see if we do indeed have authority over the demon."

Earnestly and fervently, I began to pray not only for myself, but for my friend who had concluded his sermon not understanding why the altar was empty tonight. I whispered to him what was going on and expected him to step aside. He went pale for about ten seconds, but then the fire of the Holy Spirit blazed in his eyes and he declared, "Bring her here!"

The demon possessed girl was quickly brought to the altar. The large crowd outside now curiously peered in expecting manifestations from the demon to put us in our place. We quickly bound the demon and refused to allow it to manifest itself and with authority we commanded it to leave her in the name of Jesus Christ. She was instantly delivered and cried out to God for salvation!

The missionary witnessed to her at the altar where she prayed to Almighty God for salvation through the finished sacrifice of the Lord Jesus Christ. In these brief few moments, this entire community had witnessed the miracle power given to believers in the name of Jesus as the local demoniac was delivered and gave her life to Christ!

Needless to say, early the next morning every student was present for the final day of the seminar. Sometimes at the conclusion of a seminar we discern that the people desire prayer and other times we do not. This time, however, it was unmistakably evident that all who were in attendance had come with great anticipation. These students, many of them pastors, had experienced the power of the name of Jesus for the first time, and each one came back with great expectations.

We were deluged with pleas for prayer. We began to pray and miracles began to occur. There was great rejoicing and we were profoundly amazed by the power of God. One man's arm had been withered and twisted to his chest for several months from injuries sustained in an automobile accident. After prayer, he immediately stretched forth the crippled arm and it was completely whole. He began showing everyone, lifting and waving his arm in glory to God.

When this happens, the people watching may sometimes become skeptical, including the minister who has just asked for the healing. People often wonder, "Was this ailment real or did this person just want attention?" On this

Reluctant Miracles

particular day, the man became so excited by what he had experienced that he demanded that we go with him to pray for his dying brother. This was obviously a genuine touch from God.

Often in life, the enemy backs us into a corner. None of us likes these experiences, but it is precisely at these moments that what we confess becomes what we believe. We can give in to the darkness and go home, or we can reflect the Light and watch Christ shine through us.

Chapter 15

Does Anyone

Want A Dog?

I REMEMBER AS a young pastor trying to keep up with the stack of books, videos, and literature that people thought I needed to read, hear, or investigate. I would spend countless hours trying to whittle away at the stack, only to discover that it always grew larger after each service. Finally, it became more of a hideous monster than a resource center. Since then, I have realized that most of these resources came from sincere people with the simple desire to bless their pastor in the same way they were blessed by the material. However, I have discovered that I am usually not as blessed by the resources as I am by the relationship with the one who gave them to me.

Ministers are always cautioned not to allow themselves to get too close to those to whom they minister because of the emotional pain it brings when people must leave a church. I, for one, have never been able to heed that warning. I am greatly blessed to have known and developed friendships with many great believers over the years. From Dr. Mark Rutland, I have learned a principle that has made it a little easier for me when people must move in and out of my life. He teaches that "some people are for a *reason*, some for a *season*, and others for a *lifetime*." Since learning that principle, I now try to discern each relationship that God brings into my life from this wise perspective.

I am amazed that God is never late. He always sends the right people for the right reason at exactly the right time. I remember one such example that occurred during the building of our first addition on the campus of our church. We began to construct a metal building even though none of us had any experience with this type of construction. Suddenly, an unexpected strong gust of wind stressed one of the main beams dangerously close to bending, which would have ruined the entire structure. Quickly, the men of our team joined in a circle in our parking lot and began to pray for God to send help. They prayed, "Lord, we don't know what to do. We need someone who understands this kind of project to help us. Amen."

Immediately upon the conclusion of this prayer, a stranger pulled into the church parking lot. He hopped out of his van and said, "I construct metal buildings for a living and have all the tools. We are out of work right now and I need work. Could you use me?" This gentleman faithfully shared his knowledge and tools with us and worked diligently throughout the entire project. What a blessing it was to have God send him along for just the right reason. During another building project, God sent a family to us that had access to special heavy machinery that we needed. After providing a crane for the construction project, they quickly left. I'm sure God also sent them to us temporarily for just that *reason*.

God sends other people at just the right *season*. Throughout my ministry, God has faithfully sent people with the talent needed to accomplish specific goals in a particular season of my ministry. Sometimes it was people who could raise or give money during a building program, while other times He sent people with the necessary administrative tools required for reaching the next level. One such occasion when God showed His greatness in this way was the year when our church was without leadership in our music ministry at the beginning of the Christmas season. I remember praying to God and telling Him that I so wanted to be able to have a traditional Christmas season with carols and special music, but that was not possible using pre-recorded worship music.

God quickly and faithfully answered my earnest prayer. My phone rang and much to my surprise, the call was from one of the most sought after Ministers of Music in the Southern United States. He called to say that he was being transferred into our area and asked if he could be of help for a short while. It was a fantastic holiday season with his music leadership. Then he moved on.

Sometimes, God has worked through very strange circumstances to bring these connections into my life. Years ago, one of our members began pointing out to me the need for a Spanish outreach with the growing Hispanic population of our community. Some weeks later the Holy Spirit did indeed confirm in my heart that we were to start a Spanish ministry. Therefore, I began looking for someone to help with this project, but quickly became very frustrated in the search. We were willing to start a Spanish ministry, but since none of us spoke Spanish, we were stuck waiting for someone to help. Many people wanted to use our building for their own Spanish ministry, but no one was willing to embrace the concept that we

106

did not want a separate ministry, but wanted to incorporate a part of our current ministry in Spanish.

I often tend to jump ahead of God's plan, and while I was looking and pushing for the right person to help me start a ministry, God had another avenue He was bringing into place. God often uses ways we would never have considered in order to line people up for availability to complete His tasks in His timing. Joseph came to Egypt to rule, but arrived as a slave. David was anointed King, but originally had not even been invited to the anointing ceremony. Likewise, God would use something as strange as an unruly pet and a change of staff in our school to bring the right person into our lives.

My brother and his wife engaged in a hobby with dogs for a few years. One day my sister-in-law brought me a name and phone number of a man who had contacted them about a problem with his dog. Although they never met, they had talked at length on the phone and she had learned that he spoke excellent Spanish and was the son of a missionary couple. Knowing that we needed a Spanish teacher in our Christian school and that he was looking for a job, she suggested that I might want to talk with him. At the time, there were no funds to hire a school teacher so I didn't call him immediately.

Every time I went to throw away the note with his name and phone number, God would not let me do it. For months the note lay on my desk untouched. Then one day God provided the funds and I searched for the note, but couldn't find it. I reasoned that it must have been accidentally thrown away during a cleaning session. Much to my surprise, the note soon resurfaced and I was finally able to give the young man a call. After a long phone conversation, we scheduled a time to meet and discuss our need and his ministry in more detail.

On the day of our appointment, he arrived late for our meeting which made an extremely bad first impression on me. In fact, I normally do not even meet with late arrivals. However, for some reason that day, I still agreed to see him when he arrived. When he walked into my office I was shocked because he didn't look a thing like I expected. Over the telephone I had imagined him to be a skinny, dark-skinned, preppy guy. In stark contrast to my preconceived ideas, I now stood face to face with a husky, blond-headed guy who could never be described with the word "preppy". I instantly knew he was just the right fit for our ministry.

Years later, the Spanish ministry continues to grow and disciple people for the cause of Christ. He and I have traveled together to many countries to minister the Gospel of Jesus Christ. He presents the Gospel through music, and then translates while I share about Christ. Together we stand in awe of Almighty God who faithfully draws people to Christ.

On one occasion when we were ministering together in La Entrada de Copan, Honduras, we humbly watched as approximately 250 young people prayed to receive Christ. Suddenly, I realized how blessed I was that God had once again miraculously brought exactly the right person into my life. Thankfully, this was a relationship designed by God not for just a reason, or a season, but for *life*.

I have learned to remind myself to never forget that whenever and however God chooses to provide, it is always just what I need whether I know it or not. Too many times I have limited myself because I tried to have the plan worked out in my mind to solve all my problems, and rarely did it include some chance meeting. Remember, God is gently nudging us in the right direction, so open your eyes and realize that He may have already placed what you have been waiting for right in front of you.

Chapter 16

Do Unto Others

B UT WHEN YOU do a charitable deed, do not let your left hand know what your right hand is doing, that your charitable deed may be in secret; and your Father who sees in secret will Himself reward you openly.
Matthew 6:3-4 NKJV

I think this is one of the most misinterpreted passages of Scripture in the Bible. Oftentimes, people have used this as an excuse not to tithe "openly", or in reality not to tithe at all. But a closer investigation of this Scripture reveals that this in no way refers to tithing or even to giving an offering, but rather of giving to those who are in "need". "Need" is somewhere that most of us have found, or will find, ourselves at some point in our lives. For some it is financial, for others it is the need for comfort at a time of loss, and for some it might even be support during an extended illness.

I remember the day we got the news that a dear friend and brother had just been diagnosed with cancer and was calling for prayer. He was not a member of our church, but was a member of our "extended" family of Christ. We prayed for several years for our brother and eventually he found the ultimate healing that can only be found as we are embraced in the arms of our glorious Savior.

I was so blessed to have known this man and to have been a witness of what he had sown into others coming back during his time of need. He was not what most people would have expected or gathered from their first meeting with him. He was opinionated and not afraid to share it; he was extremely head strong when his mind was set. But deep in that compact frame there was a heart of compassion and giving.

I do not know all the instances of the people who were helped during his life, but I certainly was blessed to hear of the many testimonies which were shared with me as I met the friends and family during the time of his illness and passing. As I recount this, I can only be specific about those instances that I am certain of.

I remember when my brother was trying to get started in life and he had hit a rough patch along the way. Our family was going through a shaking and finances were not something any of us had much to spread around. My brother recalls the times that Dean would stop by to bring groceries or just to make sure that his family was warm during the winter.

I was a young pastor working for $350 a month. My wife and I were spending more on the ministry than we were making. We were so excited about the upcoming birth of our first child, but we didn't have a lot of money to prepare for some of the provisions of a new baby. Dean and his wife, Janice, took us to a nice restaurant for dinner. They then blessed us with gifts for the baby. I look back on that evening as one of my fondest memories.

Our school was in need of computers but we had very little money. Dean stepped up to the challenge and blessed us not only with equipment but also with support for that equipment as well. Once I was sitting in his home when I noticed a picture hanging on their wall of the very spot I had proposed to my wife. He would not let me leave until I took the picture with me.

113

The stories could go on and on about his heart, but rather let me make a point that has stuck with me from the blessing of knowing my friend. A point I never want to forget. I watched as during his sickness people came from all around to help out, people who had once been a recipient of Dean's generosity. People were there financially, they were there to help with the kids, and prayers bombarded the Kingdom of Heaven. I even observed one day as a group of men skied down his driveway in the snow to cut fallen trees from their driveway in case his family needed to get out in an emergency.

Even though Dean is now in a better place, people are still lined up asking if there is anything they can do for this man's family. The point: his generous heart did not seek the praise of men, but rather gave in the love of Christ to others, and when the time of his need came he truly reaped what he sowed. He had done unto others as he would have them do unto him.

Chapter 17

God Is Going To
Give You A Car

I REMEMBER THE first time the Lord spoke to me and commanded me to go and deliver a "word" from Him to someone else. It would have been easier to obey if it had been an easy message such as, "God wants you to know that you are going to have a great day today!" It would not have been too difficult to deliver a message like, "Repent!" But the very first time that God gave me a word from Him for someone, He gave me a message to deliver that seemed humanly impossible that it could ever come true. I know now that God gave me this challenging word not to *test* my faith, but to *increase* my faith as He proved Himself while I watched what only the one, true, living Almighty God could orchestrate.

The Lord spoke to me and said, "Go and tell this lady that her husband is coming home." Now everyone in the church knew he wasn't coming home. He had already taken up residence with another woman. The leadership of the church had already advised her to file for divorce. Now God wanted me to tell her, "Your husband is coming home!" It would be easier for me to deliver such a message now because of my towering stature or the respect people show for my position as Pastor. However, at the time God spoke this to me, I was just a twelve-year-old kid who clearly heard God's voice.

Obediently, I walked over to this lady during church while she was praying and whispered to her, "God told me to tell you that your husband is coming home." At first she appeared a little stunned, but then a ray of hope shot from her spirit and the Scripture became manifest:

> *"...if two of you agree on earth*
> *concerning anything that they ask,*
> *it will be done for them*
> *by My Father in heaven."*
> *Matthew 18:19 NKJV*

She hugged me and cried, and I walked away wondering to myself, "What have I just done?" However, within two weeks her husband was home and I learned a valuable principle about obeying God's voice. My faith became so much greater through my twelve-year-old eyes by watching God perform a miracle so obviously supernatural.

Seventeen years later, I was standing in the reception hall of our church listening to a young family of our church talk about everything they needed, but just couldn't afford at the time. One of the things they needed was a second vehicle. As fast as they said it, I heard myself saying, "*God is going to give you a car.*" Their reply was a good, faith-filled answer, "We know God wants us to have a car and with His help we will get the financing." I replied, "No, God is going to GIVE you a car!" This time they received the word and our conversation ended. Silently, I thought, "Okay, where did that come from?" Suddenly, I felt pressured to personally make it come true. Yet, once again, God clearly and quickly demonstrated that He does not need my help in these matters.

The next morning as I entered the sanctuary, someone reached out and grabbed my arm. I turned and one of the men of our church leaned toward me and whispered, "Pastor, my wife needed a new car, so we bought one and we now have an extra car that we want to give to someone in the church."

Instantly, God reminded me of the "word" from the day before. I was so excited that after the service I called one of the elders of our church to share the story. Before I could even begin, he relayed to me that his family had an extra car that they wanted to give to someone.

Within one day's time, God had not only provided a car for them, but a choice between cars. Almost immediately, I realized God also had a purpose for the second car He provided. He does not need us to make His promises come true, but it sure is fun to watch how He fulfills them through us.

Chapter 18

The Budget

I HAVE BEEN blessed as a pastor not to have wasted an exorbitant amount of time stressing over a budget. There are pastors who are expected to spend the majority of their time raising funds instead of doing the work of an evangelist. To an extreme, some churches have senior pastors whose primary purpose is fundraising. In contrast, I have been blessed by the support of a great team and wise elders who purposely structure our planned spending significantly lower than our projected giving so as to be good stewards. Even though our budget has steadily grown, we continue to choose to practice good stewardship of God's funds by not committing to a larger budget than absolutely necessary. In this way, we have the freedom and flexibility to direct extra funds to changing lives instead of meeting a budget.

However, a budget is merely a plan and the same holds true in ministry as it does with any household budget. Sometimes there are simply unexpected costs. We have faced unplanned bills because of broken equipment, extra heating or utility costs, and various other reasons. During these challenging times, we trusted and believed that God would meet our needs and a lagging budget would soon catch back up. This was exactly the case several years ago when we found ourselves facing a decision regarding our vision of seeing lives changed.

It was December and we were $1360 BEHIND in our budget, which was a very significant amount at the time. I was scheduled to minister in Haiti. The trip had been planned for some time and all the travel expenses were paid. However, there was no money for the missionaries' support offering. We had always taken a generous offering with us to bless our missionaries, but this time common sense reasoned that perhaps we should rethink the custom for this trip because we were so far behind in the budget.

However, my dad taught me very early in life that I could never go wrong giving to missions. So, the question was not *if* we would give, but *how much* we would give. Through prayerfully seeking the Lord's guidance, we believed God directed us to give the same amount that was needed to meet the budget shortfall. Obediently, we took the specified amount to bless our missionaries. Now the budget deficit was $2720 and I was off to Haiti. God reminded me of when the apostles told the people not to give but they still insisted on giving, and I realized it really wasn't a struggle to give. It was more of a blessing to know that we were doing what was right. My team and I arrived in Haiti and began to share out of the abundance of our hearts and out of our monetary lack.

We were ministering in a suburb of Port-au-Prince, Haiti. Normally, there is no phone service in that area. However, after finishing teaching one day, I was able to receive a call from home which was definitely out of the ordinary. First, I was informed that my little daughter had been ill but was doing much better. Then they said we needed to talk about funds. Of course, my heart had been heavily weighing the decision of what must be cut to manage the deficit. They began, "Pastor, we just thought you should know that someone stopped by the church and dropped off a check for $24,000!" Needless to say, the budget was met and lives were changed by the Gospel of Christ!

"If you are really eager to give,
it isn't important how much you are able to give.
God wants you to give what you have,
not what you don't have."
2 Corinthians 8:12 NLT

Chapter 19

Provision

I T WAS DURING a time of uncertainty in my life when God began to speak to me about starting a church. As a young intern, I remember the day I stood on the platform of a large church and God spoke to me and said, "Kneel down." I protested, "Not now, Lord; this is on television and I don't want to embarrass the Senior Pastor." The Lord replied forcefully, "*I said kneel down.*" So, I obeyed and knelt and the Lord spoke to me again, "I want you to go across town to Cumming, Georgia and start a church.

Go to the women's gymnasium and ask them to let you start the church there."

I felt rather awkward walking into the ladies' tan and workout spa, but I was on a mission for God. I walked up to the owner and said, "I would like to use your place to start a church. Would you mind?" The answer was, "NO!" Feeling rather silly, I turned to leave but the owner stopped me with these words, "No, I don't mind if you start a church here! Don't you want to work out the details?" I should have known that God was up to something, but I was amazed they had agreed. I hate clichés, but I have learned the old saying is true: "If God guides, He will provide".

So, the church was started in the women's gymnasium. The little church grew and soon moved from that location to another, then to a larger one, and finally to a small rented space next to a funeral home. We were desperately looking for property when God brought a group of believers into our lives. They owned a debt-free church building furnished with pews, a sound system, and many other items they were willing to bring into a merger with our church. Once again, God had provided. During the first few years in that building, it seemed every time we needed anything from architectural drawings to curriculum, all we had to do was open a closet and there it was. The church has been, and continues to be provided for.

Then it was my turn. God began to deal with my heart that it was time for me to step up to the plate and work full time at the church. We agreed upon a salary from the church and it amounted to a whopping $350 per month. That would have been a great salary in the 1940s, or maybe even during some of the decades that followed. However, this was in the early 1990s, and that monthly salary was about the equivalent of half a week's wages. However, God said to do it, so my young wife and I stood on faith and prepared our finances.

I resigned my job at a small company and had almost completed working my notice. I was in a business one day when the owner and his wife said to me, "We need to talk with you outside." I thought it was a strange request, but I stepped outside anyway and they met me on the sidewalk. They asked me, "Would your wife be interested in a job here?" I answered, "I'm sure she would, but she is not trained for this type of work." Surprisingly, they replied, "No problem. We will train her." She met with them and they gave her the job. Not only was it her dream job that she had always wanted, but they also offered her a salary that was exactly what I had just given up to go into full time ministry. Once again, God had guided and He was providing.

The church began to grow and so did our family. It was now time to buy our first home. We purchased property and secured a building loan. We invested everything we had plus more money which we borrowed from our family. When the construction was completed, the time came for the transition from the building loan to a permanent mortgage. Just a few days before closing on the mortgage, an unexpected phone call came with disastrous news.

I was working at the church during the week when my wife called me from the bank in a nearby town. She was crying. With our car loan averaged in, we did not qualify for the mortgage. We had too high of a debt-to-income ratio, and we needed to make a great deal more money. We were at the point of losing everything. I tried to console my wife over the phone without appearing shaken myself. I asked her to drive over and meet me at the church after she left the bank. While I was waiting on her to arrive, I found myself at the altar of the church. I remember praying, "God, we didn't ask to come here, but you called us here. We need your provision now."

While I was praying, someone stopped Christina in the parking lot as she walked to our car. They were unaware of how immediate our needs were. They said, "My wife and I were praying and felt that we were to find you and give you this exact amount of money for whatever the need is. Here is the money we are to give you and your husband." It was a wad of hundred dollar bills that was just enough to pay off our car!

My wife and I moved into that house. Those who gave were not family members or even our church family, but God had once again provided supernaturally.

After we moved into the house there were still tough times. Once, when money was scarce and food was hard to come by, we opened our cabinets only to find them empty. We prayed. God's Word says that we will never have to go and beg for food. God's Word came true! Into our yard came one of the families of our church in their small pickup truck loaded down with food. They gave us so much that our cabinets were filled and we were able to pass on the blessing.

I could write for hours about how God has provided, but I will end by saying, "Even when I forget, He reminds me that He is always faithful."

Chapter 20

Walking In The Clouds

I HAVE SEEN the beaches of several places. They are unique on each ocean or sea. The Atlantic has its strong odor, and the Gulf of Mexico is known for its blue water. The Pacific is dotted with amazing cliffs as the land just seems to fall off into the water far below. The African coast is pounded by waves that make our Eastern Seaboard waves look like ripples. Beaches, even with the beauty of sunsets, are not my favorite places on earth. The mountains are what take my breath away.

Mountains in the Caribbean have been manipulated by man as the farmers have tied themselves onto stakes in order to work the fields that cascade down the cliffs on the steep sides of the mountains. There is a unique mountain in Belize that looks just like a sleeping man. The mountains of the Andes in South America are so mysterious and vast that I stare in awe while soaring high above them. I am even captivated by the small, weathered, old mountains of our own Great Smokies, a range of the Appalachian Mountains in nearby North Carolina and Tennessee. Once, while driving across these mountains with a group of teenagers, I pointed to the mountains and exclaimed, "Isn't that beautiful!" They responded quizzically, "What are you pointing at?" Of course, that answer spurned a long lecture from me about the beauty of nature.

It was on a mountain that God taught me something I never want to forget. I had traveled on a trip with a ministry team to Durango, Mexico. After finishing our ministry, we drove up to see the mountains nearby for some rest and relaxation before departing for home. These mountains were so high that I suffered from mild altitude sickness, but they were so beautiful that it was worth the pain. Like kids on a playground, we played on the mountain throwing rocks over the edge and listening for them to hit the bottom. Many times it seemed as if the rocks would never reach the bottom, and then we would finally hear a small thud. I grabbed one rock to throw it, but as I looked into my hand I noticed a scorpion perched on the rock. I quickly decided the game was over.

As I stood there gazing from the mountain, I noticed a cloud far off in the distance. This cloud was headed right for us at an alarming speed. I remember watching the cloud approach and then surround us. Although visibility was low, I remember thinking, "Wow, this is great!" Excitedly I shouted, "Guys, we are walking in the clouds!" Their reply was, "Pastor, this is not a first; down below we call this fog."

They were right, but they were also wrong. Yes, fog and clouds are similar, but fog is an obstacle and clouds are beauty. I realized that some people will always focus on the fog even when the joy of walking in the clouds is possible. Visibility may be low, but it does not have to contain us. We can choose to embrace life and live more abundantly in the clouds, or we can wander helplessly through the fog. Do you know what the major difference is? It is something I never want to forget. *Fog becomes clouds on a higher perspective.*

He maketh my feet like hinds' feet,
and setteth me upon my high places.
Psalms 18:33

131

Chapter 21

Conclusion

In Atlanta's Fox Theatre, the concert was now in full swing and the crowd was on its feet. After *tobyMac* finished the second set, I caught a clear view of Frank during the intermission. His wheelchair was the only one in the handicapped row, but he looked as happy as ever. This was possibly Frank's last big hurrah. Frank would soon be admitted to the hospital and have a feeding tube put in. We had been told that this could possibly cause rapid progression of the disease and greatly hamper Frank's lifestyle.

So, in one big, last hurrah, we, the ten fortunate, chosen friends, were privileged to attend Frank's dream concert with him. For this reason, I was delighted to be here.

While waiting for Atlanta's own *Third Day* to take the stage, someone unexpectedly announced that two audience members would be selected to spend time with the band. My heart stopped! I excitedly asked, "God, did you bring me here to witness you bless Frank like this?" The announcer then called out the names of two young people who screamed and ran to the stage. Instantly, I was furious. "God, that's not fair!" I exclaimed within myself. "These kids have their whole lives ahead of them. They will have many other opportunities. Why not Frank?" I questioned God silently.

God has His way of speaking to me. Sometimes He draws me quietly, but usually He speaks to me in the stern way required for such a hard-headed person like me. God's answer reverberated through my mind, "I will take care of Frank." I dared not get my hopes up too high, but being the "spiritually minded" person that I am, I decided to wait it out quietly until I proved myself right. Silently I waited, but inwardly I knew nothing could possibly happen now that the backstage passes had already been picked up.

The concert was good. Okay, it was great. Frank was having a blast, and to tell you the truth, so was I. Of course, I wasn't about to let my wife know or she might want me to do this again. The concert ended, the encore ended, and the crowd started to leave. Since maneuvering Frank's wheelchair through the crowd was not an easy task, we waited for most of the crowd to leave, and then we started toward the doors. Just as Frank was almost through the first set of doors, a gentleman walked up to him and said, "We would like for you to have passes to meet the band." Frank's face lit up and shone like the sun! Instantly, I was humbled and my eyes moistened when I realized that God had just "taken care of Frank"! However, I had no clue what additional blessings God had in store for Frank before we left the Fox Theatre that night.

Normally, I am one of those impatient and frugal husbands who reasons to himself, "Let's leave before the closing so we can get home and not have to pay the babysitter more money." But not tonight; this would be worth the wait. We settled down in the foyer of the Fox Theater to wait for the band. Time seemed to pass ever so slowly as the wait dragged on and on.

A message was sent to us that the band would not be able to come upstairs because of security issues, so we would have to go to the band downstairs, literally, into the belly of the beast. Everyone was escorted to the stairs to be led away when they realized that Frank's wheelchair obviously couldn't follow because this famous landmark had been constructed decades before handicapped building codes ever existed.

The staff of the Fox Theatre went into immediate action while our wait continued. Amazingly, *tobyMac* came up and personally visited with Frank. That was awesome, but I could see in Frank's eyes that he really wanted to meet *Third Day*. The Fox staff kept insisting that we continue waiting. We were unsure why, but we waited nonetheless. Finally, we were told to follow an usher who led us into the main room of the Fox and right up on stage! Most people only dream of standing on the stage of the Fox Theatre; however we, the ten "fortunate ones" were the "chosen ones" tonight! Frank rolled right onto center stage and was the star of the show!

While we were waiting, the Fox Theatre staff had been very busy. To be precise, they had been incredibly busy. Just for Frank, they had taken the loading ramps from large trucks and resourcefully constructed temporary ramps leading down into the heart of this famous old building constructed without handicap access. Miraculously, we were led all the way to the lower level through a maze of service elevators, hallways, and the temporary ramps constructed just to accommodate Frank's wheelchair.

I could have happily lived my life without ever "hanging out" with the band, but even I was bubbling with excitement now. We went through the doors and were finally escorted into the same room as *Third Day*. There was free food,

136

and no matter how hard we tried to act professional, we were all starved. While we ate, we watched in amazement as each member of the band took time to personally meet and talk with Frank. Each one autographed everything he wanted, and, of course, received from him one of his famous Frank hugs.

As we finally hurried outside to catch the last of the rapid transit trains back to suburbia, Frank rolled out onto the street that night loaded down with a stash of autographed *Third Day* treasures. He even found a guitar pick of Mac Powell's on the way out! We stopped to thank God for taking such good care of Frank when suddenly I realized this was a night

I never wanted to forget.

About the Author

Pastor Don Allen, his wife Christina, and their three children, Bethany, Zach, and Jordan, have enjoyed being a part of the ministry of The Church @ War Hill since 1992, where Pastor Don serves as Senior Pastor. In this short period of time, the ministry has become an international movement known as *Destiny Ministries*.

Destiny Ministries has a vision to proclaim the love of Christ to the entire world. With a thriving local church body, a television broadcast reaching thousands, pastoral training in the United States and abroad, international congregations, and evangelistic outreaches around the world, Pastor Don has enjoyed seeing this vision come to reality.

The greatest key to the ministry of *Destiny* and Pastor Allen is a strong sense of family and purpose coupled with an unquenched passion to see the lost come to Christ.

To contact the author, please visit the church's website:

www.warhill.com